MIGHTY MILITARY MACHINES

MILITARY HELICOPTERS

BY RYAN NAGELHOUT

 Gareth Stevens PUBLISHING

Please visit our website, www.garethstevens.com. For a free color catalog of all our high-quality books, call toll free 1-800-542-2595 or fax 1-877-542-2596.

Nagelhout, Ryan.
Military helicopters / by Ryan Nagelhout.
p. cm. — (Mighty military machines)
Includes index.
ISBN 978-1-4824-2122-4 (pbk.)
ISBN 978-1-4824-2121-7 (6-pack)
ISBN 978-1-4824-2123-1 (library binding)
1. Military helicopters — Juvenile literature. I. Nagelhout, Ryan. II. Title.
UG1230.N34 2015
623.7—d23

First Edition

Published in 2015 by
Gareth Stevens Publishing
111 East 14th Street, Suite 349
New York, NY 10003

Copyright © 2015 Gareth Stevens Publishing

Designer: Nicholas Domiano
Editor: Ryan Nagelhout

Photo credits: Cover background Ensuper/Shutterstock.com; series logo Makhnach_S/Shutterstock.com; cover, p. 1 IanC66/Shutterstock.com; pp. 5, 9, 19 Stocktrek Images/Stocktrek Images/Getty Images; p. 6 Micha Klootwijk/Shutterstock.com; p. 7 Fingerhut/Shutterstock.com; p. 10 Bernd vdB/Wikimedia Commons; p. 11 PAUL J. RICHARDS/Getty Images; p. 12 USAF/Wikimedia Commons; p. 13 Jim Lambert/Shutterstock.com; pp. 14, 15 Larry Burrows/The LIFE Picture Collection/Getty Images; p. 16 LOUISA GOULIAMAKI/AFP/Getty Images; p. 17 USMC/Handout/Getty Images; p. 18 JAY DIRECTO/AFP/Getty Images; p. 21 MARWAN NAAMANI/AFP/Getty Images; p. 23 filo/E+/Getty Images; pp. 25, 26 Jordan Tan/Shutterstock.com; p. 27 Susan Walsh/Getty Images; p. 29 Noel Celis/AFP/Getty Images; p. 30 Darren Brode/Shutterstock.com.

All rights reserved. No part of this book may be reproduced in any form without permission in writing from the publisher, except by a reviewer.

Printed in the United States of America

CPSIA compliance information: Batch # CW15GS: For further information contact Gareth Stevens, New York, New York at 1-800-542-2595.

CONTENTS

The Copters	4
Hover and Slide	6
On a Tether	10
Sikorsky R-4	12
The Huey	14
Sea Stallion	16
Chinook	18
Apache	20
Black Hawk	22
Osprey	24
Copters Today	28
Inside an Osprey Helicopter	30
For More Information	31
Glossary	32
Index	32

THE COPTERS

Helicopters are amazing flying machines. They fly differently than airplanes, which are built with wings to help them fly. Helicopters use spinning blades, called rotors, on top of the cockpit to lift off the ground and fly. The US military uses many different helicopters all over the world.

INTEL REPORT

Helicopters are also called rotorcraft.

HOVER AND SLIDE

Helicopters can hover, or hang, in place in the air. They move differently than airplanes when they fly. While airplanes can only move forward, pilots can move a helicopter in any direction! A helicopter can move both forward and backward. It can even move side to side.

INTEL REPORT

Pilots move a helicopter in any direction by turning the angle of its rotors.

Each branch of the military uses helicopters for different things. Marine Corps helicopters are landed on boats and used around water. The US Army uses helicopters to move troops and fight in wars. Some helicopters are even armed with **weapons** and used in attacks.

INTEL REPORT

Helicopters can also lift things high into the air like a crane does!

ON A TETHER

Igor Sikorsky made one of the first working helicopters. Called the VS-300, it took flight on September 14, 1939. The helicopter was **tethered** during its flight, which lasted just a few seconds. Soon helicopters were made that could safely travel from place to place.

VS-300

INTEL REPORT

The word "helicopter" comes from Greek words that mean "spiral wings."

SIKORSKY R-4

The first US Air Force helicopter was the Sikorsky R-4. First flown in 1942, it could fly up to 75 miles (121 km) per hour and reach up to 8,000 feet (2,438 m). The US Air Force ordered more than 100 R-4 helicopters from Sikorsky's company.

SIKORSKY R-4

INTEL REPORT

One member of the military called the R-4 the "eggbeater" after its first official flight.

13

THE HUEY

One of the most popular military helicopters is the Bell UH-1 Iroquois. Called the "Huey," the UH-1 was **developed** in the 1950s and used during the Vietnam War (1955–1975). The Huey moved troops and **cargo** as well as attacked from the air.

INTEL REPORT

The Huey was often used to take hurt troops away from the fighting.

SEA STALLION

The Sikorsky CH-53, or Sea Stallion, was one of the most popular helicopters in the US Navy. First used in 1967 in Vietnam, it flew up to 195 miles (315 km) per hour and had a crew of 3.

INTEL REPORT

The Sea Stallion was taken out of service in 2012.

17

CHINOOK

Chinook helicopters first flew in 1962. They have two big rotors that work together to help them fly. Chinooks can carry up to 11 tons (10 mt). They have room to carry 44 troops or 22 **stretchers**.

INTEL REPORT

Many helicopters, such as the Chinook, are named after Native American tribes.

APACHE

The AH-64, or Apache, is an attack helicopter. It's loaded with missiles, rockets, and a **cannon** to fire on many types of targets. First flown in 1975, the Apache uses special **radar** to find enemies and **launch** attacks.

INTEL REPORT

The Apache can fly up to 176 miles (283 km) per hour.

BLACK HAWK

The Sikorsky UH-60 Black Hawk was first used in 1979 and still flies in the US military today. The army's Black Hawk has a crew of 4 and can carry 2,640 pounds (1,199 kg) of cargo or 11 troops.

INTEL REPORT

Twenty-five different countries use Black Hawk helicopters all around the world.

OSPREY

The V-22, or Osprey, is a very special helicopter. It has wings with two rotors that can actually turn. The Osprey takes off like a helicopter, then its rotors turn down, and it flies like an airplane!

INTEL REPORT

The V-22 is also called a tiltrotor helicopter.

The V-22 can hold up to 24 troops and carry up to 20,000 pounds (9,080 kg). It can also tow up to 15,000 pounds (6,810 kg) of cargo. The Osprey is good at landing on aircraft carriers, which are huge ships that act like floating airports.

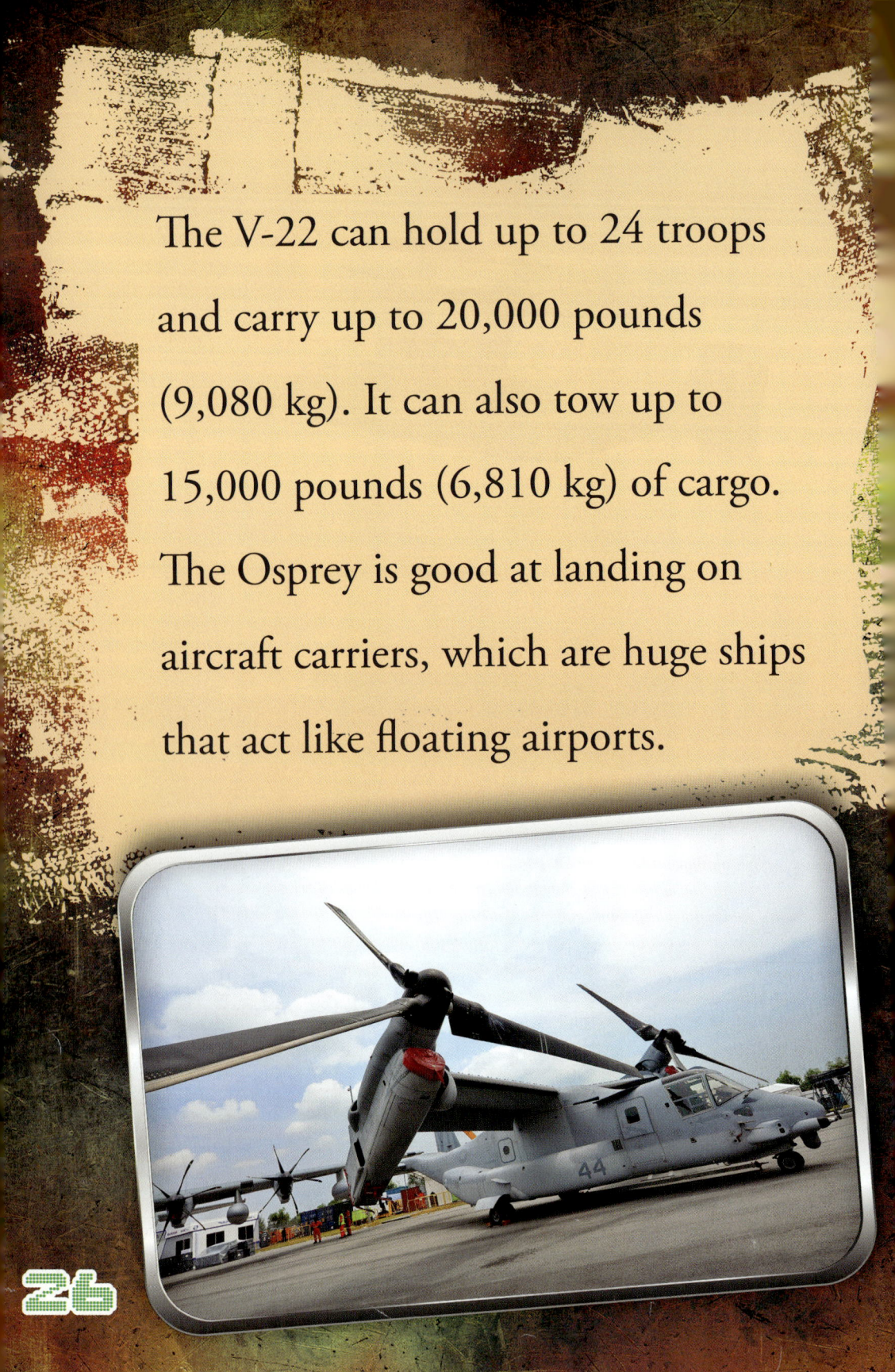

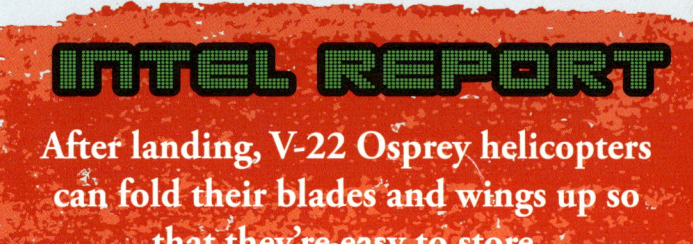

INTEL REPORT

After landing, V-22 Osprey helicopters can fold their blades and wings up so that they're easy to store.

COPTERS TODAY

The newest military helicopters are some of the coolest aircraft to ever fly the skies. The newest model of the Sea Stallion is called the King Stallion. It started flying in 2014 and is the most powerful military helicopter ever made!

INTEL REPORT

The King Stallion, or CH-53K, will replace many Sea Stallions over the next few years.

INSIDE AN OSPREY HELICOPTER

PROROTORS

COCKPIT

CARGO BAY

FOR MORE INFORMATION

Books
Bodden, Valerie. *Helicopters*. Mankato, MN: Creative Education, 2012.

Peppas, Lynn. *Military Helicopters: Flying into Battle*. New York, NY: Crabtree Publishing, 2012.

Von Finn, Denny. *Apache Helicopters*. Minneapolis, MN: Bellwether Media, 2013.

Websites
Evolution of the Sikorsky Heavy Lift Helicopters
sikorsky.com/StaticFiles/Sikorsky/Heavy-Lift-Timeline/index.html#&panel1-1
Follow the evolution of the CH-53K King Stallion on the official Sikorsky website.

Helicopters
militaryfactory.com/aircraft/military-helicopters.asp
Learn more about military helicopters on the Military Factory website.

Military Aircraft
bellhelicopter.com/Military/Military.html
Find out more about military helicopters made by Bell.

Publisher's note to educators and parents: Our editors have carefully reviewed these websites to ensure that they are suitable for students. Many websites change frequently, however, and we cannot guarantee that a site's future contents will continue to meet our high standards of quality and educational value. Be advised that students should be closely supervised whenever they access the Internet.

GLOSSARY

cannon: a large, heavy gun

cargo: goods carried by a plane or helicopter

develop: to create over time

launch: to push forward

radar: a machine that uses radio waves to locate and identify objects

stretcher: a cot or bed used to carry a sick or injured person

tether: to tie to a line that limits movement

weapon: something used to fight an enemy

INDEX

AH-64 20
Apache 20, 21
Bell UH-1 14
Black Hawk 22, 23
blades 4, 24, 25, 27
CH-53K 29
Chinook 18, 19
Huey 14, 15
King Stallion 28, 29
Osprey 24, 26, 27, 30
rotors 4, 7, 18, 24, 25
Sea Stallion 16, 17, 28, 29
Sikorsky, Igor 10, 12
Sikorsky CH-53 16
Sikorsky R-4 12, 13
Sikorsky UH-60 22
V-22 24, 25, 26, 27
VS-300 10

J 623.746 NAG

Nagelhout, Ryan.

Military helicopters

JUL 1 5 2015

MARY JACOBS LIBRARY
64 WASHINGTON STREET
ROCKY HILL, NJ 08553